UNANIMOUS PRESENTS THE UNOFFICIAL STORY OF

Anna
Kournikova

UNANIMOUS PRESENTS THE UNOFFICIAL STORY OF

Anna Kournikova

Karen Farrington

Contents

Introduction

Think of Russia's female athletes and the image of bulging arms, square shoulders and something one step away from womanhood comes to mind. Likewise, talk of lady tennis players evokes images of someone strapping and Amazonian with questionable sexuality. Russian tennis player Anna Kournikova has shattered these stereotypes – and how.

Kournikova with Gabriela Sabatini, the Argentinian tennis player who is also a popular pin-up.

Just one look at this svelte, stylish, athletic young woman makes you realise that the mould for modern sportswomen has been fashioned very differently of late. A new breed of player on court, exemplified by Kournikova, has led to a fresh throng of fans mobbing the sidelines. They are young, male and unashamedly vocal in support for their heroine. With Kournikova on court it is cool to drool from the stands.

The queen of the cropped top has got this army of young men in the palm of her hand, with her warm-up sessions drawing more enthusiastic supporters than other players' main matches. A flash of her green eyes, a flick of her blonde hair and a glimpse of her long, long legs are enough to make most hot-blooded men swoon. She makes the response to Argentinian Gabriela Sabatini, eleven years her senior, who preceded her as a tennis pin-up, appear to be a ripple to her own tidal wave. Sports writers from the intellectually challenged British daily newspapers have dubbed her 'Cor!nikova' as a direct response to her sex appeal.

Yet Kournikova is more than just a kitten on the court. She's capable of some awesome tennis shots – although she doesn't always live up to expectations, as gloating headlines on the sports pages are keen to relate. 'Kournikova proves pretty erratic.' 'Still striving to live up to the hype'. 'Kournikova caves in.' Cynics might discern an air of smug satisfaction that someone so pretty and powerful gets some on-court comeuppance.

Beautiful, yes, talented, too. But Kournikova possesses another quality that has put her firmly at the top of the popularity stakes among tennis fans today. She has bountiful charisma. Not just her face but her very being makes heads swivel in the biggest crowds. She has the ability to laugh easily, which is always attractive, but there's more to her allure than that.

'It's not just her looks,' testifies one sports writer. 'It's her style, her presence. You can't teach that. It's like having a sense of humour.' The cameras love her. While others suffer with 'off' days, Kournikova has yet to be photographed looking anything other than gorgeous. Whether her face is rapt with concentration, joyful in victory or irritated by press intrusion, it always holds the same wide-ranging appeal.

So far a major tennis title has eluded her. There have been other titles bestowed upon her, however. At 17 she was voted into the world's top 50 most beautiful people by *People* magazine. More recently she was deemed the most clickable female personality on the Internet. A poll of 1,000 Internet users aged between 18 and 24 from across the UK found they were most likely to visit websites on

'It's not just her looks …it's her **style,** her **presence.** You **can't teach** that. It's like **having** a sense of **humour.'**

which she starred. Runner-up was actress and model Elizabeth Hurley. Some 18,000 web pages spread over at least 36 different sites are devoted to Kournikova.

But make no mistake. She is wholeheartedly devoted to tennis and the quest for a significant trophy burns within her. Undoubtedly she enjoys the media attention, the commercial sponsorship and the adulation. Yet it is the dream of supremacy in tennis that drives her on. The rest is gravy.

Her attempts on court have been publicly derided. Certainly, while her instincts at the net are superlative, the accuracy of her serve could be considerably improved. However, critics appear oblivious to the fact that she has yet to reach 20 – when most Wimbledon champions achieve greatness when they are more

Their devotion is never in doubt. Kournikova's army of fans are eager to display their strength of feeling. Lovestruck calls ring out constantly when Kournikova is on court.

Left Kournikova signs herself simply 'Anna K'.

Below So far a Grand Slam title has eluded Kournikova, although she remains determined to rectify matters as soon as possible.

mature in age and experience. Martina Navratilova was 21 before her first Wimbledon triumph, while Britain's Virginia Wade was a veritable veteran at 31 years old. And Gabriela Sabatini, so fondly remembered by male tennis fans everywhere, only achieved one Grand Slam title before her retirement from the game in 1996, at the age of 26.

It's a fact that isn't lost on Kournikova, who claims she is relatively unconcerned about the lack of a significant singles championship trophy in her cupboard. 'I think about it, of course, but it's not like 'I have to, I have to'. I know my time will come.' On another occasion she admitted the major obstacle in her path to greatness when she said: 'I have control over all balls but I have to learn to win. With top level tennis your mental strength is everything. You can win if you have that.'

Whether or not she ever does strike gold with a Grand Slam title, she has become one of the wealthiest women in sport, with earnings estimated in excess of 1,700,000 dollars in prize money alone. Her overall fortune is estimated by Forbes magazine to stand at 11 million dollars. She is one of the five most sought-after female athlete endorsers in the world. While other top-ranking women players earn big prize money, no woman in the sport today peaks her earning power.

One
Childhood

Anna Kournikova is Russian-born but largely American-bred. She came into the world in Moscow on 7 June 1981, just after Pope John Paul II was shot and wounded in St Peter's Square and shortly before Prince Charles married Lady Diana Spencer in St Paul's Cathedral in London.

Above The bond between mother and daughter is close. Alla Kournikova has chaperoned Anna since the tennis prodigy left Russia for the US, at the age of 10. Today they choose to spend plenty of time together.

In tennis terms, it was the end of an era. Before Kournikova was one month old, Bjorn Borg's record-breaking run of 41 singles victories at Wimbledon – including five consecutive titles – was bought to an end by John McEnroe in a nerve-wracking final. It was the same year that Chris Evert Lloyd beat Hana Mandlikova in the Wimbledon women's singles final. She lifted the trophy for the third time.

As a baby Kournikova was blissfully unaware of the momentous political changes occurring in her homeland. Soviet president Leonid Brezhnev died in November 1982 and Yuri Andropov was his successor. Andropov, a former chief of the feared secret police, the KGB, was a tough nut but even he must have quailed in the face of the tremendous domestic difficulties facing the superpower.

Right Alla Kournikova was a 400 metre runner in her youth. She's married to Sergei, a wrestler turned university lecturer who works in Moscow.

Within 15 months Andropov had died, giving way to Konstantin Chernenko – who lasted little more than a year.

In 1985, the year that Kournikova celebrated her fourth birthday, reformer Mikhail Gorbachev took charge in the Soviet Union. He authored the policy of perestroika, which accelerated the process of democracy and helped to dismantle the tools of repression that had loomed large in Russia since the Bolshevik Revolution of 1917. Ultimately, he was replaced by Boris Yeltsin, who continued a relentless process to demolish the Iron Curtain.

While these were exciting times, they were not without problems. The mood of optimism was shadowed by uncertainty, with food shortages and a fluctuating rouble. Ordinary people like Kournikova's parents lived in some measure of trepidation. There was talk of coup and counter-coup. The Cold War, although thawing, was not over. Residents of Russia were left to second-guess the actions of the USA and other Western countries.

Kournikova's father, Sergei, was a professional wrestler turned academic. After studying for a PhD he became a lecturer at the University for Physical Culture and Sport in Moscow. Her mother, Alla, was a 400-metre runner. Their home was a spartan two-bedroom flat in Moscow.

Even as a tot, Kournikova showed tremendous promise on court. Her power and poise continued to grow during her childhood years.

Even as a tot Anna, their only child, showed promise as a tennis player. The Kournikovas sold their TV set in order to supply their blonde and bubbly daughter with a tennis racquet and then they invested further in some training. Aged five she was delivering some impressive forehands, complete with topspin. Soon she had won her first championship match. 'I'm a bit like Cinderella… I got to go to the ball,' Kournikova later observed.

Parents everywhere are delighted to spot and nurture precocious talent in their offspring. In countries where the political situation is uncertain and cash is short, the desire is all the more urgent.

Sue Livingston, president of the British Women's Tennis Association, explains why girls from countries which once lay behind the Iron Curtain strive harder than their Western counterparts. 'From an early age, girls from the old Eastern Bloc have a mental toughness that ours don't have. I don't blame individual players, it's just not in our culture to be totally driven. If kids don't want to follow a regime or a programme, they aren't forced to. Money is definitely an influence on the Continent. In the smallest satellite tournaments on the European circuit, a first round loser gets $98. That's nothing here and I don't think our players are remotely motivated by it, but in Bulgaria or Slovakia $98 buys a lot of product.' Thus top-flight women's tennis players have emerged in droves from former Communist countries.

It all helps to explain why Alla Kournikova was determined to make the most of her daughter's burgeoning skills. By the age of seven, Kournikova was enrolled at the renowned Spartak sports academy in Russia. It was there – where she proved herself able to competently return balls across the net with a remarkable degree of consistency – that her talent was spotted. Gene Scott, the publisher of Tennis Week magazine, alerted the tennis scouts back home in the States.

At the age of 10, Kournikova left Moscow with her mum to join

Kournikova honed her skills at the Nick Bollettieri Tennis Academy in Florida, alongside other up-and-coming players.

the Nick Bollettieri Tennis Academy in Florida, where players Monica Seles, Pete Sampras, Mary Pierce and Andre Agassi revealed their early promise. The Academy, on Longboat Key, which started in 1977, caters for more than 2000 full-time students from over 40 different countries, as well as running summer camps.

While her contemporaries back in Russia piled on the furs in the face of another brutal winter, Kournikova was soaking up the sun after a major change in lifestyle. In landlocked Moscow, the luxuries had been few and the privations many. 'When I first came to America I could not believe all the things I saw. I wanted to have those things but I knew that I had to work hard to buy them,' she said. In Florida, the Atlantic Ocean represented the boundless

While other teenagers were concerned with pop music, school studies and spots, Kournikova concentrated on perfecting her tennis shots in a hectic schedule of practice sessions and matches.

freedom that for years Russia had been denied. She still lists the beach as one of her favourite places.

In 1992, when she was just 11 years old, Kournikova became the youngest athlete ever signed up by International Management Group, the largest sports management company in the world, which now also owns the Nick Bollettieri Academy.

At first sight she appears every inch a gum-chewing, cola-swigging surf chick. Nevertheless, the emotional ties with Mother Russia remain strong. Since turning professional in October 1995 at the age of 14 she has represented her country – albeit speaking with a Miami twang – and has worked hard to bring it glory on the court.

Kournikova was just 11 years old when she was signed by IMG, the largest sports management company in the world. Her potential for superstardom was inescapably obvious.

Two
Anna Kournikova
The Player

Kournikova has a double-handed backhand to die for. Her forehands are strong and her drop shots effective. On top form she can serve at 111 miles per hour. Kournikova has been said to lack poetry when she is in motion but she is extremely athletic – and that counts for quite a bit these days.

She prefers grass courts to clay. 'It suits my game. I can serve and volley. It's aggressive – that's what I like.' All in all, her talent is formidable – but is, alas, far from foolproof. Her reputation for squandering set points and desperate double faults is as great – if not greater – than for pulling off against-the-odds victories.

Still, Kournikova, among other leading women players, has reversed the fortunes of women's tennis. Just seven years ago Holland's Richard Krajicek described women tennis players as 'lazy, fat pigs'. His reason for this was not made clear at the time, but the statement certainly holds no water today.

No longer are fans queuing to see male tennis stars playing power tennis from one baseline to the other. It is the women players who are bringing in the crowds, not just for the pure enjoyment of the game but also because Kournikova, Martina Hingis, Monica Seles and the Williams sisters, Venus and Serena, are more appealing, exciting and, often, explosive at the moment. The feuding, bitching and bickering that has gone on between women players often colours the sports headlines. The lure for the spectator – to see if any of the enmity spills over into the game – remains great.

Georgina Clark, Director of European Operations for the Women's Tennis Association Tour, puts it another way. 'The women's game has a nice mix at the moment of quality tennis players and interesting personalities. The modern women are increasingly fit and well trained, which makes them more and more preferable to watch than the men.'

It must also be noted that watching Kournikova yields the additional thrill of seeing her tuck her second service ball in her knickers! This one simple and unconscious action alone is probably responsible for making a huge impact on the numbers rolling in through the turnstiles.

Despite this, women competing at major tournaments like Wimbledon still get paid less than their male counterparts. Only the

'The women's game has a nice mix at the moment of quality tennis players and interesting personalities. The modern women are increasingly fit and well trained, which makes them more and more preferable to watch than the men.'
– Georgina Clark.

23

US Open has complete parity. Tim Henman, the British number one, feels that for men to be paid the same as women would be unfair, given that men play five rather than three sets in a match. He said: 'I think they should worry about getting their own tournaments at a bigger and better level and then worry about the grand slams… if they are still saying they want more in the grand slams, I think that's probably a bit greedy.'

Wimbledon's organisers insist that the differences in prize money reflect the gulf in gate money between women's and men's tennis – a view that is currently looking rather dated. A spokesperson for the Women's Tennis Association gave its position: 'What do people prefer when they go to the movies, a boring three-hour movie or a superb 90-minute production? You want the best movie you can see.'

Monica Seles added her weight to the argument for equal payouts. 'Everywhere we go crowds are up, TV ratings are up, interest is up. Women's tennis deserves more.' Recently John McEnroe waded into the argument about the fairness or otherwise of the situation. 'Pay female tennis players what they're worth. The women are carrying the promotional load and bringing fans through the turnstiles. They should be paid accordingly.'

No one has upped the profile of the women's game in the past five years more than Kournikova – even if her detractors insist that the acres of press coverage are given for the wrong reasons. It is duly thanks to her, then, that the issue of women's prize money has been brought high on to the agenda.

Kournikova launched on to the top tennis circuits like a comet. Her glittering trail of success, it seemed, would go on forever. The women's tour is divided into five levels, with the Grand Slams at the

Kournikova is famous for tucking her second service ball in the leg of her knickers, oblivious to the sensation it causes among her devoted following.

Right On court her athleticism has never been in doubt. However, for Kournikova service has sometimes been erratic, which leaves her vulnerable in crucial matches.

Next page A magnet to the crowds, Kournikova is nevertheless paid less than male players in most of the tournaments she plays. The issue of parity continues to cause controversy in the game.

Kournikova spends six hours a day on court in practice sessions, in a bid to achieve her dreams of securing a Grand Slam title.

top. Tournaments are then rated from Tier One to Tier Four. The bigger prize money is attached to the more prestigious events. Players also win ranking points through their results, which affects what position they occupy in the tennis world rankings.

Kournikova won a host of junior championships before turning professional in October 1995, which gave her a reputation for imminent greatness prior even to picking up a racquet in a pro match. In 1996, aged just 14, she was the youngest player ever in the Federation Cup and helped Russia to victory over Sweden. The same year she was named as the WTA Tour Most Impressive Newcomer.

During her second year on the WTA Tour she defeated three top ten players – Iva Majoli, Arantxa Sanchez Vicario and Anke Huber – when she herself was much lower in the pecking order of women's tennis. She complained that her style was being cramped by an age ruling that restricted the number of matches she was permitted to play during her young teenage years. 'How am I supposed to compete against the top players if I can only play a certain number of tournaments? It is difficult… to play a top player without having more match practice. This keeps me back and hurts my ranking,' she argued. When she did play, she racked up some remarkable results.

The high point of her career as a singles player is acknowledged to be the 1997 Wimbledon tournament, when she progressed to the semi-finals, finally losing to the eventual champion, Martina Hingis. It was a splendid debut in the tournament, repeating a first-timers' feat achieved only once before, by Chris Evert in 1972. She admitted that the unexpected success was like a dream come true. The campaign began on Centre Court with a convincing win over Chanda Rubin. Other 16-year-olds might have been intimidated by the hallowed environs. If Kournikova was daunted, she didn't let it show. Keeping her nerves firmly in check, she forged ahead to victory, to the delight of fans in the crowd. In an interview after her fourth-round win over Helena Sukova – at 32 precisely double Kournikova's age – she once again rued her lack of experience. 'I think I have to get experience by playing. Other than that, (improvement) really comes with years of playing.'

But there were those watching her meteoric rise who feared that the fiery talent was at risk of being reduced to a flicker rather than a flame. After her performance at Wimbledon when she was 16, Russian journalist Vitali Yakovenko said: 'She is very talented but I fear it might be difficult to find the right path with her. There are too many managers and too much media attention for a girl of this age.'

His words proved strangely prophetic. The golden girl of tennis appeared suddenly to start to falter, almost as if additional maturity was accompanied by the burden of self-doubt. She still achieved noteworthy victories but there were an increasing number of evident aberrations. One sports writer has likened her as a player to the girl in the nursery rhyme who, 'when she was good, she was very, very good, and when she was bad she was horrid.'

There have been some astonishing upsets. In the first round of Wimbledon in the summer of 2000, Kournikova came up against French player Sandrine Testud. Fans watched in disbelief as Kournikova went from a five games to two lead in the second set to lose seven games to five. She went on to win the match, but the performance proved that while the body is willing, the mind is sometimes weak.

In January 1999 her performance in the Australian Open brought forth howls of derision from observers. She double-faulted 31 times in her second-round match against Japan's Miho Saeki, twice at match point. Although Kournikova won the match, the flaw of her game lay exposed for all to see. She can occasionally be psyched

Even during her run of success at Wimbledon in 1997, Kournikova publicly regretted her lack of match experience, which she felt hindered her chances.

Above and right Kournikova pictured with Martina Hingis, her former doubles partner, with whom she won the Australian Open title in 1999.

out when she should be psyched up.

But signs that she is overcoming these difficulties are emerging. In August 2000, when she was ranked eighteenth in the world, she defeated the highly rated Lindsay Davenport in the Acura Classic, doing so after her opponent won the first set in twenty minutes. Afterwards Kournikova told journalists: 'I've really improved mentally. I've gotten more experienced. I'm not getting down on myself so much if I lose a point. I don't look back, I just look forward.'

Davenport freely admitted her mistake. 'I had some chances early in the second set that I didn't take. Once you let a player like that back into the match she starts to feel more comfortable and hits better and better.' Davenport, by the way, is a full six inches taller than Kournikova, and most of that is translated into the belting serve that typifies her game.

Despite the occasional chasms in form, the Russian commanded a position in the top ten of the world rankings for six weeks in the early part of 2000. She has spent much of her professional career haunting the top ten. There is clearly considerable substance to her game and those statistics knock the stuffing out of many of the glib criticisms leveled against her.

Kournikova has known more success as a doubles player. Partnering Martina Hingis, she won five doubles titles in 1999 including the Australian Open. When Kournikova teamed up with Martina Hingis, after the latter dropped her previous partner Jana Novotna, it was the volatile Hingis who called the new pairing the 'Spice Girls of the tennis world'. The partnership with Hingis has now ended, with Hingis citing 'personal reasons' for the split.

Kournikova found some success, too, with her mixed doubles partner Jonas Bjorkman, who is Swedish-born but is now living in Monaco. Together they were runners-up in the Wimbledon championships of 1999 after entering at the last minute. In the Australian Open in 2000 they reached the semis again. For Bjorkman, it seems that playing with Kournikova is a major distraction – not because of her stunning looks but for the overreaction of her male fans. 'It's amazing to stand on the court with her and see so many guys going nuts,' he says.

Billie Jean King, who was herself a tennis sensation, said: 'Being a beautiful woman is a lot like being a tennis player – you know the best of it has to end when you're still young. To be both, as Anna is, can be hard. After all, from the age of ten she's heard two things over and over – how beautiful she is and how great a player she is.'

Christine Truman-Jones, a British tennis prodigy of the late 1950s, believes that life in the camera lens is probably harming Kournikova's game. 'Needing to worry about shoulders back, bust out and tummy in all the time can't be good for her tennis,' she said.

Pam Shriver believes she is under the same pressures as Martina Navratilova was during her career. 'Martina was the sport's most talked-about lesbian. Anna is the sport's most talked-about beauty queen… which leaves both more vulnerable than you'd imagine. 'Anna has the game – powerful strokes, a hard serve, athleticism. She can be mentally tough. She served 31 double faults in the second round of the Australian Open last year and rallied to win. She's a pro. She puts in the work. You don't just plop down on this earth with that body.'

Nathalie Tauziat, who testified that tennis was Kournikova's true passion, said: 'I can speak without jealousy or nastiness because I like her. She is fun and rather nice, even if she unfortunately does

'You don't just **plop** down on this earth with that **body.'**

According to Pam Shriver, being the sport's most talked-about beauty queen perpetuates plenty of pressure for Kournikova.

not show respect to everyone. 'In my opinion she's already had enough of being worshipped. Enough of always being told that she's the prettiest, the best this, the best that… What she wants is to finally win a tournament and be recognised for that, or play in a Grand Slam final, and it's for that reason I like her a lot.'

Her early form was undeniably impressive. When Kournikova was 15, Steffi Graf freely admitted that the Russian had the ability to be a top player. 'But she has things to work on. She gets impatient when she doesn't end the point quickly. She hits her forehand very flat and needs to have a safer shot to use when she is under pressure. She is not going to outhit bigger girls right now and needs to use other shots to open up the court. She is not as powerful as Venus Williams but she has a strong body. The question is more about her stamina. She puts so much energy into her shots that sometimes they seem to take a lot out of her by the second set. But Anna definitely has potential.'

Virginia Wade, Britain's former champion, was filled with optimism about Kournikova's chances before the 1998 Wimbledon tournament. 'She may be only 17 but do not be fooled by the pretty face, the model features and the swishing pigtail. This girl is really tough, she will come to the net on grass, she is clever, she puts a lot of pressure on her opponent and she is ambitious. Very ambitious.

'I see it in her swagger, there is a self-composed assurance about her, she is still very young and there are no inhibitions in her game. She reached the semi-finals at Wimbledon last year and although she took only five games from Martina Hingis I thought she was always in with a chance... She is anxious to do well, you can see that. Sometimes she just winds herself up a little bit too much, but I would rather notice that in a young player than someone who is flat and has to work on building themselves up into a frenzy.' In the event, Kournikova was forced to withdraw after suffering from torn ligaments following a fall in a quarter-finals match at

Kournikova winces with pain while her wrist is bandaged after an injury during the Mexican Tennis Open Doubles, 2000.

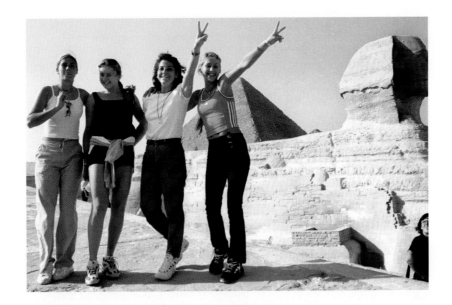

Visiting the pyramids in Egypt, Kournikova – with other young players – takes a break from the rigours of the tournament circuit. Although dedication to the game means missing out on some aspects of youth, there are some tremendous advantages too.

Eastbourne that year – a match in which she defeated Steffi Graf.

Helena Sukova was grudging in her admiration of Kournikova after the latter beat her at Wimbledon. From a previous generation of players who largely escaped press attention, she remarked that some fared well with it while others went under: 'If they can survive, it tells you that they must be strong characters.'

However, Kournikova has also been branded an 'arrogant diva' by fellow female players. One claimed there were always happy faces in the locker room among fellow female players when she lost a match. 'She's just a pretty girl who gets all the attention,' said another. 'We all like each other except Kournikova, no one likes her,' said another. She has been described as 'pretty and horrid as opposed to merely pretty horrid'. Former coach Nick Bollettieri is quoted as remarking: 'Anna doesn't have an idol… she's her own.' (Equally, he concedes that she has yet to reach her potential.)

Still Kournikova remains calm in the volley of personal criticism. 'Tennis is an individual sport, not a team sport, and rivalry is absolutely normal – a perfectly human response.' She is not the only

Kournikova remains cool about off-court criticism levied by other players, which she puts down to natural, instinctive rivalry.

With her every move scrutinised in the press and each stroke of her game pored over by the pundits, Kournikova has become public property and must strive to keep an iota of privacy and a sense of dignity.

player to face hostility from established players. Martina Hingis, who also entered the tour with a fanfare, was ignored by fellow competitors when she made her professional debut in Zurich in the autumn of 1994. More than that, they went out of their way to cheer her opponent. Like Kournikova, Hingis stayed serene.

Monica Seles comments, 'Anna has things that the rest of us don't have so yes, some of the players are envious of her. But others who know her like her.' Martina Navratilova, who won 18 Grand Slam titles, has questioned the driving force propelling Kournikova. 'Anna is in good shape to compete but she isn't willing to get into the trenches. She doesn't need to and it's akin to a kid with rich parents... I don't think she has the motivation – I haven't seen it yet – but she does have the talent. As yet, she does not have the hunger. Maybe she will get it. Maybe she will get annoyed enough with these comments and will get going.'

At the moment Kournikova remains in the shadow of Switzerland's Martina Hingis. Encounters between the two make excellent viewing and are far from predictable. 'Every time I play Martina it is different. It is new emotions every time,' said Kournikova. Only when Hingis became a professional was Kournikova recognised as the world's top-ranking junior player.

Kournikova is capable of beating Hingis. She proved it in the quarter-finals of the 1998 German Open – even though Hingis had won each of the four matches they had previously played. Realistically, Kournikova said afterwards: 'I played much better than I did before against her and she was probably not ready for that. It was difficult playing against her because she has a lot more experience than I do, so I just tried to concentrate on my game and be aggressive and take control of the points early.' The result was telling for Hingis, who only a day before the match had said: 'I know (Kournikova) can play but she's never shown it against me.' However, Hingis can usually be relied upon to gain the upper hand.

Competition in the women's game is fierce, and Kournikova continues practising hard to increase the strength of her shots. She is still keeping a major title in her sights.

Competition in the women's game has rarely been fiercer. The Williams sisters are dominating the scene at present. As a singles player, Venus Williams triumphed with Olympic gold in Sydney. With sister Serena, she picked up a further gong in the doubles. Venus Williams also challenged Lindsay Davenport, for two years the most consistent player, for the Wimbledon crown in 2000 – and won.

Sisters Venus and Serena Williams celebrated the millennium in style, winning a clutch of singles, doubles and Olympic titles between them. Like Kournikova, they came from humble beginnings.

The story of the Williams sisters bears the same fairytale quality that Kournikova's does. They came from the Los Angeles ghetto, the most unlikely breeding ground for tennis greats. They first wielded their racquets on shabby neighbourhood courts beset by graffiti and vandalism. But their father Richard saw potential in the girls (the youngest two of his five daughters) and persevered.

Now they are mighty figures on the women's circuit – in more ways than one.

Venus Williams stands at six feet one inch, compared with Kournikova's five feet eight inches and, at 169 pounds, she weighs some 46 pounds more. This could explain why Williams recorded the fastest ever serve in WTA history in 1998 at Zurich – an amazing 127mph. The physical deficits are hard to make up for a player like Kournikova. Nevertheless, she continues her punishing training programme in pursuit of some extra power behind her shots. For at least six hours a day, she hammers balls around a tennis court. In addition, she tops up with a session in the gym. She possesses a grim determination to get to the top and it is this which influences her behaviour if she has failed on court. 'If I've played poorly I'm seriously bad news for at least an hour. If I were someone else,

When she has completed hours of slamming a tennis ball around the court each day, Kournikova retires to the gym for more body toning to improve her strength and stamina.

After losing on court, Kournikova's usual happy demeanour deserts her and she becomes morose, even sullen.

I wouldn't want to talk to me after a defeat.'

On court she dresses quite demurely, often in a simple gold-coloured dress. She avoids the fashion statements made by the Williams sisters, perhaps realising the effect that revealing extra tracts of flesh might have on her fans. Invariably her splendid hair is swept back into a braid, which gets up an impressive whiplash momentum of its own during games.

Physically a strong girl, she's nevertheless suffered her fair share of injuries. Practising for the Canadian Open in August 1999, she succumbed to a stress fracture in her right foot which kept her out of the game for three months. In May 2000 she tore a ligament in her left ankle as she competed in the second round of the German Open. Despite convalescence on the sunny Spanish isle of Mallorca, she was still not fully fit for the summer schedule.

Kournikova is locked into the upper echelons of the World Tennis Association Tour, during which the major titles are played for. Her continuing lack of success has prompted some to question the

'If I were someone else, I **wouldn't want** to **talk to** me after a **defeat.'**

wisdom of this. Would she be better off playing – and winning – in smaller tournaments? It's not a course of action that she favours. 'If I'm going to play a smaller tournament and beat somebody in the finals that ranks 100, I don't think it's going to bring me a lot of confidence.'

Accusations that she is some kind of tennis freeloader are particularly hurtful. Those who know her well put her commitment to the game beyond doubt. Look at any photograph of her on court and in action. Kournikova's face is a picture of concentration. She is absorbed entirely in the match and in each nuance of the ball.

But the ability to play tennis amounts to much more than a gift from the gods. It's a career that demands hard work, lots of it. On numerous occasions Kournikova has made that commitment of endurance and intensity. She is prepared to roll up her sleeves and work at it, even after unexpected defeat. After losing to a less experienced player in the American Open she said: 'I just have to go back and work and prove my consistency. I know that I can play well. I've shown it before. I've beaten a lot of players, all five number ones in the last 10 or 15 years. I just have to go back out there and work on my consistency.'

'To be **Number One** at anything takes hard work and I'm working **hard. Believe me,** I'm working hard.'

On another occasion, when her serve had let her down badly, she said: 'The serve, like any other shot, can come and go. I am just going to have to go back and work on it.' At a third press conference she declared: 'To be Number One at anything takes hard work and I'm working hard. Believe me, I'm working hard.'

Her present coach, Eric Van Harpen, is guarded in his response to the entourage that clings to Kournikova, including photographers and fans. 'She's the best looking of all the players and, just like Sabatini was, she is always the focus of attention. Although I would like to see less. It is difficult to speak my mind when she is so surrounded by all these fans.'

Kournikova has even been accused of hogging the limelight at the expense of other young Russian players. Elena Dementieva, the Olympic finalist, became the first Russian woman to reach the US Open semi-finals in 2000. The achievement went almost unnoticed in the media.

Coach Olga Morozova said: 'We are very proud of Elena, she has a great heart, she is a fantastic fighter. Her game is getting better and better. She doesn't get much publicity, not as much as she deserves.

'Dementieva has done everything right and worked very hard for everything she has achieved. She earned all she has by playing tennis. We're giving her full publicity in Russia but it is very difficult in the US to get publicity if you don't have the right marketing people behind her.'

Kournikova is not afraid of hard work. After her serve deserted her at the American Open, she pledged: 'I am just going to have to go back and work on it.'

Three
Anna Kournikova
The Superstar

It's the face that has graced scores of magazine covers – including *Esquire, Vogue* and *Cosmopolitan*. The complexion is youthful, tanned and healthy. Those lips cushioning even, white teeth are full. The eyes smoulder with a knowing expression. Cascades of golden hair frame this flawless face. Kournikova is glowingly glamorous.

The seventh day God created "ANNA.K." n.t.m.

Faithful fans stick by Kournikova through thick and thin, delighted by her buoyant personality and her assertive tennis. They are thrilled by her victories and stoic in her defeats.

She smiles readily, flirts outrageously and is not hindered by modesty or timidity. Indeed, she exudes self-confidence in the manner she talks and the way she walks. From the age of 12 she has possessed a self-assurance way beyond her years.

Undeniably she has star quality. In March 1998, after a victory in the State Farm Evert Cup competition, Kournikova strode over to the umpire's chair, seized the microphone and asked the crowd to sing 'Happy Birthday' to her mother, Alla. She proved herself to be more than merely a calendar girl.

She has no illusions about her celebrity status. After being introduced to the Spice Girls in 1998, she declared: 'It was a big deal for them, not for me.' They were about the biggest band in Britain at the time.

Breathtaking conceit, according to some. For others the bold, blandly delivered statements are the symbols of a survivor. Public perception of Kournikova is framed by newspaper articles written by correspondents who have often felt a frost from the tennis player as biting as that which crisps the Red Square in February.

She refuses to be coaxed or cajoled into answers and never bends in the onslaught of questions an inch further than she intends to. Journalists in her company after a stunning on-court victory find her eloquent and upbeat – although still economical with words. Sports writers who plague her with questions following a defeat form their opinions from the sullen, petulant figure in front of them. She can be brief, mute or even hostile. Kournikova herself admits she is hell to be with for at least an hour after losing a match. The following dialogue between sports writer and tennis star, which took place after a defeat in the third round of the US Open in 2000, is not untypical.

Q: How disappointing is it?
A: Well, of course, it's disappointing.

Q: But how much? How do you feel?
A: Disappointed.

Q: Are you in shock at all?
A: I'm just disappointed.

The terse exchange reveals how Kournikova refuses point blank to pander to the press. She's likely to respond in monosyllables or even ignore questions altogether if it suits her mood. Yet she knows full well that even when she slaps them down, the reporters will return for more.

Kournikova admits she tires of the constant questioning from the press. At one Wimbledon press conference she was asked seven times about the identity of her boyfriend. Seven times she repeated

Above Relentless press attention affects not only Kournikova but all those around her. In this picture, ice hockey player Sergei Federov gets a taste of the limelight.

the same answer, 'no comment'. 'People form their opinions by seeing me on magazine covers and reading about me. I read about me, too, and sometimes I appear as if I've come from another planet, or I'm learning about a twin sister,' says Kournikova.

The constant buzz of press attention is wearying but, unashamedly ambitious, Kournikova knows full well that she is not just a top tennis player, but also a star. Kournikova's aspect on the issue of press intrusion is tinged with realism. 'You don't think people would go on about my looks if I was number 500 in the world instead of number 12 do you? Anyway, as I keep telling everyone, you can't blame me for looking like this on purpose. I have things about me that are not perfect, but I am a tennis player. There are thousands of beautiful women but how many have the ability to play tennis, to be a personality?'

Right 'People form their opinions by seeing me on magazine covers and reading about me,' says Kournikova. Yet when she reads about herself, she often doesn't recognise the character profiled in articles.

Already experienced as a model, Kournikova has announced her keenness to become an actress when her career as a tennis player has finally ended.

She has also made no secret of the fact that she wants to become an actress when her spell as a tennis player is over. There's been plenty of speculation about her cashing in on her appearance. Certainly, her shapely figure – she weighs in at about 123 pounds – could take her places, either on the big screen or as a model.

Already she promotes sports bras for makers Berlei – with the provocative slogan 'only the balls should bounce'. Wisely, she negotiated a deal in which she was not required to pose in her underwear. Indeed, she refused even to take off the jacket masking the exquisite lines of her figure. The only stipulation in her contract was that she was photographed tossing some tennis balls in the air. At a press conference organized by Berlei she was asked whether she would rather be beautiful or the world Number One. 'Can't I be both?' she sparred coquettishly.

The media interest that she commands has inspired some spin-off criticism. Dr Precilla Choi, of Keele University, recently condemned the hype that she believes is deterring women from pursuing sport to improve their health. 'At Wimbledon Kournikova was hailed as one of the best role models for women's tennis and this is a woman who isn't as good as Mary Pierce. Women in sport are still being valued more for what they look like than their performance.'

In her book, *Femininity and the Physically Active Woman*, Choi claims the expectations of women when they take up sport are raised with the high profile of athletes like Kournikova. When their appearance fails to change, women tend to drop out of sport – even though they were reaping the benefits of improved health.

Writer Victoria Coren, who once cast doubt on the talent of Kournikova in a British newspaper, is not convinced that the sight of a slim Kournikova keeps women out of the gym. 'Last time I said that people made too much fuss over the Russian blonde I got the kind of letters you'd expect if you confessed to drowning kittens for

Kournikova has become known as a cropped top queen, baring her midriff to sensational effect.

a thrill. Men from all over London sent helpful analyses of my jealousy. Half of them began "If you were pretty yourself" or "If you ever had a boyfriend"... But that's because it's men, not women, who lose perspective over Anna. And her face is actually her fortune. All tennis players have great bodies: Kournikova's legs have nothing on Steffi Graf's. But Anna gets the front pages for her button nose, big eyes and shiny hair. Women are not so stupid that they think going to the gym will give them a prettier face. Nobody has stared in disappointment at the mirror after an hour of Pilates

Captivating on court, Kournikova proves
she can be just as spellbinding off it.

and said: "Oh, I thought my nose would get smaller." So it's irrelevant that Anna Kournikova is more famous than Mary Pierce. The sportswomen are good role models, physically anyway, because they stand there as glowing, muscled proof that exercise does give you a better body.'

France's Nathalie Tauziat, in her book *Les Dessous du Tennis Feminin (The Underside of Women's Tennis)* wrote: 'If Anna appears to have a life as exciting as a film star, it is because those around her are busy building a myth while cultivating her mystery, and she adds her bits too.

'When she stopped travelling to Russia to play in the Federation Cup I heard it was because the Mafia wanted to kill her. Later Anna told me she had simply been injured. Everyone around her competes with each other to sell her image as the Lolita with the perfect body. Who else but Anna could inspire a TV programme on the trouble male line-judges have in concentrating when they are seated behind her?'

It was American television that dubbed her 'Lolita', the teenage temptress created by Russian writer Vladimir Nabokov in his book of the same name. Speculation about her every move is rife. How long does she spend in front of the mirror? Who is her date tonight? Is she pulling a publicity stunt to attract more press coverage? The response from Kournikova is truculent. 'I can't change and I won't change. People misunderstand what I'm about. I'm just being me. Every time I do anything, it's translated as attention-seeking. If I change my hair it's because I want to. I don't sit down and plan it all out.'

In one of her more philosophical moments, Kournikova shrugged off the penalties of life in the spotlight. 'Maybe it's fair, maybe it's not fair. It's just the way it is.' Comments that the press bombardment was hurting her game and that she was 'too sexy' did seem to hold water, however. She herself became keen to burst the bubble of

Above Americans know Kournikova as 'Lolita', the teenage siren with the ability to bewitch admirers created by Vladimir Nabokov in his book of the same name.

Left Kournikova has been photographed across the globe, on court and off. The results are always inspiring, giving a fresh dimension to the word photogenic.

Away from tennis, Kournikova is just like any other girl her age, enjoying TV, basketball, and chatting to her friends.

glamour. 'I cannot help the way I look,' is the message she has freely given on numerous occasions. 'I'm here to be a tennis player and I want people to focus on my game. That's what matters.' When she's asked why she thinks she is the focus of so much attention she advises the questioner to ask reporters and camera crews rather than her. They do not, after all, attend at her personal invitation.

In 1998 Kournikova switched management teams with a view to taking the froth out of her image and replacing it with something altogether more focused and hard-nosed. Her obligations to Adidas and Berlei remained, but many of the other commercial distractions were filtered out. Phil de Picciotto, from Advantage International, the Virginia-based agency that she joined, explained the new approach. 'The process was a bit out of control, so what we said was that until you have a story to tell, let the on-court story be the only one. Let attention shift naturally back to your tennis. If she wasn't a very good tennis player she wouldn't be the subject of all this attention. But unless the environment is managed quite carefully,

the attention will be an impediment to her… We want her to maintain a career perspective that starts, continues and ends with tennis.' Thereafter it became all but impossible to squeeze more than two sentences out of her.

That Kournikova takes pride in her appearance is beyond question. She admits that seeing herself on a hoarding in a giant-sized advert gives her a measure of satisfaction. 'First and foremost I'm a professional tennis player, but to be honest, yes, I do enjoy being up there on a billboard the size of a house. 'People ask me sometimes why I think it's necessary to look good on court. But surely a tennis court is like a stage and I have to express myself every way I know. Why should I have to look ugly just because I'm an athlete?'

In an apparent bid to shake the 'dumb blonde' tag, she recently appeared in an advertisement that discussed stocks, shares and bonds. 'Everyone is amazed. They ask me: 'You really know about that stuff or did you just learn it for the commercial? I tell them I wouldn't do it unless I understood and had an interest.'

The flipside of fame has also come to dog Kournikova. Full-length nude shots of

'to be honest, **yes,** I do **enjoy** being up there on a **billboard** the size of a **house.'**

'Let the on-court story be the only one,' said Kournikova's new management team in 1998. Since then Kournikova has attempted to curb contact with the press and focus entirely on tennis.

Away from the hectic schedule of tournaments and practice, Kournikova has developed a passion for many other activities, including a recent devotion to Formula One Racing.

Kournikova were posted on the Internet during Wimbledon 1999. They were fake, of course. The urge to exploit her extraordinary looks was clearly overwhelming. Serial streaker Mark Roberts, of Liverpool, dashed stark naked across court Number 14 at Wimbledon in 2000 where Kournikova was playing and somersaulted over the net. Written across his chest was the slogan 'Only the balls bounce', a reference to her sports bra endorsement. The tennis superstar was left to bury her head in her towel as Roberts was pursued by security men.

There's a brash side to Kournikova's nature that occasionally surfaces and looks none too pretty. She is capable of out-and-out rudeness. Bollettieri once asked her to leave his academy after one of her outbursts was directed at a coach. She redeemed herself with an apology, but still occasionally remains prone to throwing racquets around the court in frustration.

Some of her off-court behaviour has recently smacked of spoilt superstar. In March 2000 the player and her mother were on an American Airlines flight to Miami when a crew member requested her to put her miniature Doberman Pinscher dog in its carrying case, as per the flight rules. Eventually the pilot was called to intervene. Police sent a report of the incident to the FBI, which later decided to take no action.

However, consider her complex background and the outbursts appear more in context. She's a girl who had nothing – and now has it all. At the age of 15 she was still deeply conscious of her Russian roots. 'I don't care what kind of hotel I stay in or what kind of car I have. Anything is fine with me because I came from Russia where we had nothing. So to me, to be able to play on the pro tour and travel and have this life is good enough for me.'

Knowing the shortage of material goods and even food in Russia – she visits as often as she can – it makes it hard to respect the consumer durables that are so readily available to her now. Nick

Always the target of cameramen armed with long lenses, Kournikova has few moments in which to let her hair down without the fact being reported in banner headlines to the world.

Above Like many teenage girls, Kournikova had an ambition to swim with dolphins. For a superstar of her stature, it's not difficult to arrange.

Right Kournikova has the instincts of a cat on the court. Even this tiger is willing to show her respect!

Bollettieri pondered: 'Sometimes Anna must be lost. She never had a childhood. She must wonder what it's like to live a normal life.'

'What is normal?' retorted Kournikova. 'That kind of life everybody talks about as 'normal' wouldn't be normal for me. From the age of five, when I first played tennis, that's all I wanted. I was so happy on the tennis court. I can't think of anything better. People say I missed out on childhood but I don't think so. I have had the greatest time, playing tennis, winning matches, doing everything I loved. I am a very energetic person. I have never been able to sit still, so it is good that I have had something to concentrate on.'

Thanks to Bollettieri, her ebullient self-confidence and straight-talking ways were largely muzzled. 'I've told Anna and others that you have to learn to have manners out on the tour. If you're going to say things that anger the other players, you're only going to make them want to beat you more. Then they'll make sure to play their best against you and make your job harder.'

In her spare time, Kournikova is much like other young women, listening to music, reading books, watching TV (The Tonight Show with Jay Leno and Melrose Place are reputed to be her favorite shows.) Outside tennis she enjoys watching NBA basketball and ice hockey. Lithe and tanned, she looks undeniably stunning when she dons one of her cropped tops and bares a tantalising inch or two of slender midriff. Her favorite color is black and it appears from her extensive wardrobe regularly. She avoids alcohol. If Anna looks squeaky-clean, it is because she showers four times a day, following every training session and gym workout.

Fans send her gifts – of jewellery and toys – in addition to mailbags full of letters and photos. The attention is ceaseless. However, Kournikova – who signs herself simply Anna K. – has some measure of affection for the adolescents and adult men who fill stadia to watch her in action.

Of her faithful fans she says: 'It's good that they're watching tennis

Despite the trappings of success, Kournikova is keen to enjoy herself when the opportunity allows, just like other teenagers.

and not out on the street.' Whether the constant lovestruck calls of encouragement that ring out at crucial moments are a help or hindrance, she doesn't say. Her effect on ball boys working in tournaments has not gone unnoticed. Now they are warned not to stare when she is on court.

The bond between mother Alla and daughter Anna remains strong, so much so the pair act more like sisters. There have been wild rumours about Alla Kournikova and the effect she has on her daughter. Nick Bollettieri is said to have banned her from attending training, so forceful was her personality. Word that Alla was one of those fearsomely ambitious parents who ruthlessly steered the careers of their vulnerable offspring didn't ring entirely true, however. She has lived and travelled with her daughter since they left Russia together, and they are as close as any parent and child can be. The number of glances that Kournikova throws towards her mother during a match is proof of that. However, Anna does not have a personality that is easily subdued. Nor will she be led along paths she does not want to tread. The notion that she is bullied or manipulated in any way by her mother is risible.

A crowd-pleaser even when she isn't playing,
Kournikova signs programmes for fans.

Four
Love Life

Anna Kournikova is legendary for her one-liners, which have left the vast majority of her male admirers weeping in her wake. 'You can't afford me,' she is often quoted as saying, sweeping imperiously past a gaggle of gawky, gawping fans.

Ice hockey player Sergei Federov has been Kournikova's companion for years. When asked what it was like to go out with Kournikova he replied: 'A learning experience, that's for sure.'

It's more likely that the put-down was a jest that she has repeated in good humour. The story appears to have begun when Kournikova stayed at a hotel in Eastbourne, southern England, in the tournament that precedes Wimbledon. It is at Eastbourne that fans risk life and limb and cling to the chimney of a house that overlooks the tennis courts in order to catch a glimpse of their golden girl. A young waiter there fell under her spell. 'She's always laughing and joking. She seems really nice,' he told reporters. 'I asked her to marry me and she gave me this big smile and said, "I don't think you could afford me".'

Sergei Federov, striker with the Detroit Redwings ice hockey team, has been romantically linked with Kournikova on a number of occasions in the past few years. The two sportspeople share Russia as their mother country, although Federov – ten years her senior – defected rather than departed. Their families were friends when Kournikova was still a girl. It was Federov who allegedly sent her no fewer than 200 roses as proof of his undying love. He did so even though he knew full well the penalties of dating the star. When asked what it was like going out with Kournikova he said: 'A learning experience, that's for sure. Sometimes not very fun but that's what it is.'

At the time Alla Kournikova played it cool, even when Federov became a constant fixture during Kournikova's practice sessions. 'I don't think Anna's private life is anybody's business. The media make such a big deal of everything but sometimes they get the wrong impression. They see friends, it doesn't mean it's her boyfriend.'

Kournikova has apparently dated other sports stars, namely ice hockey player Pavel Bure, of the Florida Panthers, Ecuador's top tennis player Nicolas Lappentti and Australia's on-court sensation Mark Philippoussis. Publicly she insists the men whose names are linked to hers are only pals. Of Philippoussis she says: 'We're just good friends – and have been since we played in juniors in Florida together.'

Gossip-mongers went into overdrive when they heard that Bure, another Russian, had proposed to Kournikova in a Miami restaurant in March 2000, presenting her with a £650,000 diamond ring. However, Russian newspapers reckoned that Bure and Alla Kournikova had fallen out and the relationship was at an end. Alla was accused of transforming her daughter into a 'money-making machine'. Speculation is rife that Alla has exaggerated or even invented stories to get her daughter's name into the headlines.

There have even been suggestions that Kournikova has dated the Brazilian footballer Ronaldo. In a rare departure from the normal 'no comment', Kournikova spoke out during the Wimbledon of 1999. 'The last time I saw (Ronaldo) was the only time I saw him, at the French Open last year, when we were introduced to each other and that's all. That's the one and only time I ever saw him, and ever talked to him.' At the time she insisted she did not have a boyfriend, although Sergei Federov was very much in the picture. Says Kournikova: 'The media get too deep into your private stuff. It may seem like a mystery to you but really, I am just trying to have some things stay private.'

However, there have been some tantalizing facts which she has let slip. At bedtime she wears only Issey Miyake perfume, she teases. And she has been at pains to reassure reporters that her virginity remains intact.

She's a typical Gemini, the star sign of the twins. That means she's secretly searching for the soulmate who will make her feel complete. In personality she is a typical Gemini – fleet-footed, nimble, intuitive and fond of her freedom. The positive aspects of her horoscope mean that she is charming, youthful, spontaneous and quick-witted. The sign is also associated with impatience, a non-committal attitude and something of a dual personality. Geminians

Any boyfriend of Kournikova's has to share her passion for tennis. Federov fits the bill.

71

'Boyfriends have to understand me and my needs… I separate my
professional and private lives.'

are compatible with the majority of the other eleven star signs but horoscopes warn against relationships with Scorpio and Capricorn. Hard luck, Scorpio and Capricorn suitors!

When she has spoken of her ideal man, Kournikova rates sense of humour and an outgoing personality as essential. She makes it clear that any potential partner will have to fit in with her lifestyle. 'Boyfriends have to understand me and my needs. They have to know what I want out of my life and about my strict regime. I go to bed at 10pm and not later. I separate my professional and private lives.'

Above When footballer Ronaldo was said to be an admirer Kournikova denied it.
Above left Pavel Bure, another ice hockey player, has also been romantically linked to Kournikova.

Five

Where From Here?

Given the relentless attention of the paparazzi, the fawning fans, the rich opportunities yielded in the commercial sector – alongside the pressures of playing top level tennis – perhaps Kournikova's biggest challenge is not to burn out before her 21st birthday.

She's already set to prove a degree of staying power by outlasting Carling Bassett, another blonde beauty who once galvanized the media. In 1982 Canadian-born 'Darling' Carling was the top-ranked junior in the world. When she turned professional in 1983, sportswriters were speculating about the greatness she would achieve. In the event she retired from competition in 1988 at the age of 21 without having won a major title. If Kournikova wishes to mimic anyone it must surely be Chris Evert, the all-American princess of the court.

She's not the only hopeful who is being frustrated in their ambitions at the moment. Tim Henman, like Kournikova, has a devoted following of fans and yet has delivered much less than he promised. Before Wimbledon 2000 he revealed the down-to-earth optimism that might equally apply to Kournikova. 'I'm a firm believer that if you keep putting yourself in these situations, sooner or later it will go your way.'

Tennis has dominated her existence for as long as she can remember. More than a mere obsession, it is the very fabric that makes up her life. Only when she is sleeping, she claims, is her mind away from the game. Throughout her first five years of professional tennis she has perched on the brink of 'the big one', the Grand Slam title which every player craves. She's not about to give up on the dream of tennis greatness.

Early in her professional career she pledged: 'I'm not going to let anything distract me. Everyone thinks everything has come easy to me but it hasn't. I've had a lot of pressures on me and handled them.' She has never wavered from her stated aim.

The quality that Kournikova has – to press buttons inside people and provoke a response – has taken her into the limelight. This trait is one that the major companies love to capitalise upon. Ulf Dahlstrom, from Adidas, tries to verbalise the appeal. 'Who else crosses all the boundaries – the whole spectrum, all over the world? Who ever did before her? Anna is everything.'

She has melted the attitude of even Richard Krajicek, well known for his disdain of the women's game. 'I hate women's tennis. But I could watch Anna for two hours, even playing shuttlecock.'

The new millennium appeared to offer fresh impetus to Kournikova and she notched up some encouraging results in 2000. In Sydney she reached the semi-finals of the tennis competition, with victories over Sabine Appelmans, Jennifer Capriati and Alexandra Stevenson to her credit. She was also a semi-finalist at 2000 Paris Indoors and also at Scottsdale. It was enough to edge her into the world's top ten rankings at number nine, a career best. Her results at

Observers have speculated about Kournikova's commitment to tennis. This is despite a steady and discernible improvement in her game. Her dedication has never faltered.

her favourite tournament, the French Open, were disappointing, but she was still in the process of recovering from injury.

She forged a successful doubles partnership with French player Julie Halard-Decugis, winning the title at the first event of 2000, held in Gold Coast, Australia. The Grand Slam singles title proved as elusive as before, however, and her failure to secure one continues to prompt criticism of 'under-achievement'.

Despite the strut and the polished words, there's a vulnerability about Kournikova. Poised on the edge of superstardom, she needs a convincing tennis triumph to prevent her from tumbling into oblivion. One tournament organiser elaborated on the dilemma that faces her: 'If she won just one major she would become the most famous female athlete of all time. She's that special.

'On the other hand, if she doesn't win, when does it all start to pale? Right now she is the beauty who plays tennis. But what if she becomes the beauty who never wins at tennis? Is this as big as it gets?'

She might find comfort from a surprising source. In her book 'Being Myself', Martina Navratilova put it this way: 'It's good always to have something to overcome, whether you're in sports or any other field. In the past I was put down because I wasn't winning every tournament in sight, but now I use that criticism for motivation.'

At present Kournikova remains the brightest star of the circuit, if not in tennis terms then certainly as an international figure of the future. It seems inconceivable that she will fade into obscurity when her tennis dreams are exhausted. The crowds will still flock to see her, wherever she goes. Newspapers and magazines the world over are still content to feed their readers a diet of Kournikova snaps and snippets. The Kournikova cult shows no sign of abating.

'If she won just one major she would become the most famous female athlete of all time'

Index

Published by Unanimous Ltd

12 The Ivories, 6–8 Northampton Street, London N1 2HY

A CIP catalogue record for this book is available from the British Library.

Editor: Nicola Birtwisle

Design: Staziker Jones

ISBN: 1 903318 38 6

Printed in Italy

1 2 3 4 5 6 7 8 9

Picture credits

Page 2 Clive Brunskill/ALLSPORT; 4 Allsport/ALLSPORT; 6 Clive Brunskill/ALLSPORT; 8 PA Photos/EPA;
10 Daniel Moloshok/ALLSPORT; 11 top Clive Brunskill/ALLSPORT; bottom M. David Leeds/ALLSPORT; 12 Al Bello/ALLSPORT;
14 Simon Bruty/ALLSPORT; 15 Clive Brunskill/ALLSPORT; 16 Simon Bruty/ALLSPORT; 17 Clive Brunskill/ALLSPORT;
18 left Clive Brunskill/ALLSPORT; right Clive Brunskill/ALLSPORT; 19 Simon Bruty/ALLSPORT; 20 Neil Munns/PA Photos;
22 M. David Leeds/ALLSPORT; 24 Neil Munns/PA Photos; 25 Clive Brunskill/ALLSPORT; 26–27 Clive Brunskill/ALLSPORT;
28 top Gary M. Prior/ALLSPORT; bottom Clive Brunskill/ALLSPORT; 29 Darren England/ALLSPORT;
30–31 Clive Brunskill/ALLSPORT; 32 Toby Melville/PA Photos; 33 PA Photos/EPA/Greg Wood; 35 Alex Livesey/ALLSPORT;
37 PA Photos/EPA; 38 Clive Brunskill/ALLSPORT; 39 PA Photos/EPA; 40–41 Al Bello/ALLSPORT; 42 PA Photos/EPA;
43 Gary M. Prior/ALLSPORT; 44 PA Photos/EPA/APA/GEPA/Ingrid Gerencser; 45 Clive Brunskill/ALLSPORT;
47 Clive Brunskill/ALLSPORT; 48 Mark Dadswell/ALLSPORT; 50 PA Photos/EPA/Greg Wood; 51 PA Photos/EPA/Robyn Beck;
52 Gary M. Prior/ALLSPORT; 53 Clive Brunskill/ALLSPORT; 54 Fiona Hanson/PA Photos; 55 Phil Cole/ALLSPORT;
56 Gary M. Prior/ALLSPORT; 57 Clive Brunskill/ALLSPORT; 58 Jamie McDonald/ALLSPORT; 59 Clive Brunskill/ALLSPORT;
60 left PA Photos/EPA/William West; right PA Photos/EPA; 61 Fiona Hanson/PA Photos; 62 Clive Brunskill/ALLSPORT;
63 top Gary M. Prior/ALLSPORT; bottom PA Photos/EPA; 64 Darren England/ALLSPORT; 65 Darren England/ALLSPORT;
66 Darren England/ALLSPORT; 67 Clive Brunskill/ALLSPORT; 68 Fiona Hanson/PA Photos; 70 Clive Brunskill/ALLSPORT;
71 Mike Hewitt/ALLSPORT; 72 PA Photos/EPA; 73 Clive Brunskill/ALLSPORT; 74 Jed Jacobsohn/ALLSPORT; 77 Tom Hevesi/PA Photos.